Meet the
DALLAS
COWBOYS

By
ZACK BURGESS

NORWOOD HOUSE 🏠 PRESS

CHICAGO, ILLINOIS

NORWOOD HOUSE ![house icon] PRESS

P.O. Box 316598 • Chicago, Illinois 60631
For more information about Norwood House Press please visit our website at
www.norwoodhousepress.com or call 866-565-2900.

Photo Credits:
All photos courtesy of Associated Press, except for the following: Black Book Archives (6, 7, 15, 18),
Crane's Potato Chips (10 top), Topps, Inc. (10 bottom, 22, 23), NFL Pro Line (11 top),
Pinnacle Brands (11 middle), Pro Set (11 bottom).

Cover Photo: James D. Smith/Associated Press

The football memorabilia photographed for this book is part of the authors' collection. The collectibles used
for artistic background purposes in this series were manufactured by many different card companies—
including Bowman, Donruss, Fleer, Leaf, O-Pee-Chee, Pacific, Panini America, Philadelphia Chewing Gum,
Pinnacle, Pro Line, Pro Set, Score, Topps, and Upper Deck—as well as several food brands, including
Crane's, Hostess, Kellogg's, McDonald's and Post.

Designer: Ron Jaffe
Series Editors: Mike Kennedy and Mark Stewart
Project Management: Black Book Partners, LLC.
Editorial Production: Lisa Walsh

LIBRARY OF CONGRESS CATALOGING-IN-PUBLICATION DATA
Names: Burgess, Zack.
Title: Meet the Dallas Cowboys / by Zack Burgess.
Description: Chicago, Illinois : Norwood House Press, [2016] | Series: Big
    picture sports | Includes bibliographical references and index. |
    Audience: Grade: K to Grade 3.
Identifiers: LCCN 2015022485| ISBN 9781599537320 (Library Edition : alk.
    paper) | ISBN 9781603578356 (eBook)
Subjects: LCSH: Dallas Cowboys (Football team)--Miscellanea--Juvenile
    literature.
Classification: LCC GV956.D3 B86 2016 | DDC 796.332/64097642812--dc23
LC record available at http://lccn.loc.gov/2015022485

288N—072016
Manufactured in the United States of America in North Mankato, Minnesota

CONTENTS

Words in **bold type** are defined on page 24.

The Cowboys take the field.

4

CALL ME A COWBOY

The Dallas Cowboys are known as "America's Team." They have loyal fans everywhere. Year after year, the Cowboys put talented players on the field. They always play exciting football. That is why fans across the country root for the Cowboys as their "hometown" team.

TIME MACHINE

In 1960, Dallas got its own team in the National Football League (NFL). Coach **Tom Landry** guided the Cowboys to two Super Bowl wins in the 1970s. Dallas won the championship three more times in the 1990s. Troy Aikman, Emmitt Smith, and Michael Irvin led those teams.

Quarterback Troy Aikman won three Super Bowls.

There are no bad seats in the Cowboys' stadium.

BEST SEAT IN THE HOUSE

The Cowboys' stadium is one of the largest in the world. It also has a huge video screen that hangs over the field. In all, the stadium can hold more than 105,000 fans. That also makes it one of the loudest home fields in the NFL.

SHOE BOX

The trading cards on these pages show some of the best Cowboys ever.

ROGER STAUBACH

QUARTERBACK · 1969–1979

Roger led the Cowboys to the Super Bowl four times. He was called "Roger the Dodger" for the way he dodged tacklers.

TONY DORSETT

RUNNING BACK · 1977–1987

Tony seemed to glide right past opponents. In 1982, he set a record with a 99-yard touchdown run.

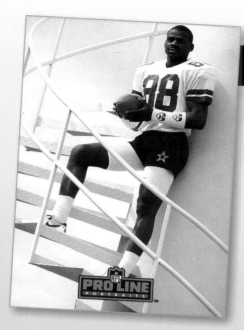

MICHAEL IRVIN

RECEIVER · 1988-1999

Michael was a fearless pass-catcher. He held on to the ball no matter how close tacklers were to him.

TROY AIKMAN

QUARTERBACK · 1989-2000

Troy followed in Roger Staubach's footsteps. He led the team to three Super Bowl victories in four years.

EMMITT SMITH

RUNNING BACK · 1990-2002

Some experts thought Emmitt was too slow and small. He ended up as the NFL's all-time rushing leader.

THE BIG PICTURE

Look at the two photos on page 13. Both appear to be the same. But they are not. There are three differences. Can you spot them?

Answers on page 23.

13

TRUE OR FALSE?

Tony Romo was a star quarterback. Two of these facts about him are **TRUE**. One is **FALSE**. Do you know which is which?

1. In 2006 and again in 2013, Tony threw five touchdown passes in one game.

2. Tony's father and grandfather were both real cowboys.

3. Tony made the **Pro Bowl** three times from 2006 to 2009.

Answer on page 23.

Tony Romo takes charge for the Cowboys.

15

Cowboys fans love to get rowdy.

Go Cowboys, Go!

The Cowboys have fans all over the world. That includes countries where football isn't played. On game days in Dallas, just about everyone wears silver and blue. Fans treat the Cowboys like kings. Many players stay in the Dallas area after they retire.

ON THE MAP

Here is a look at where five Cowboys were born, along with a fun fact about each.

1   **TONY HILL · SAN DIEGO, CALIFORNIA**
Tony was nicknamed "The Thrill" for his great speed and amazing catches.

2   **DON PERKINS · WATERLOO, IOWA**
Don was one of the NFL's top running backs when he played for Dallas.

3   **DEMARCUS WARE · AUBURN, ALABAMA**
DeMarcus led the league in **quarterback sacks** twice as a Cowboy.

4   **DREW PEARSON · SOUTH RIVER, NEW JERSEY**
Drew was named an **All-Pro** receiver three times.

5   **TONI FRITSCH · PETRONELL-CARNUNTUM, AUSTRIA**
Toni led the Cowboys with 104 points in 1975.

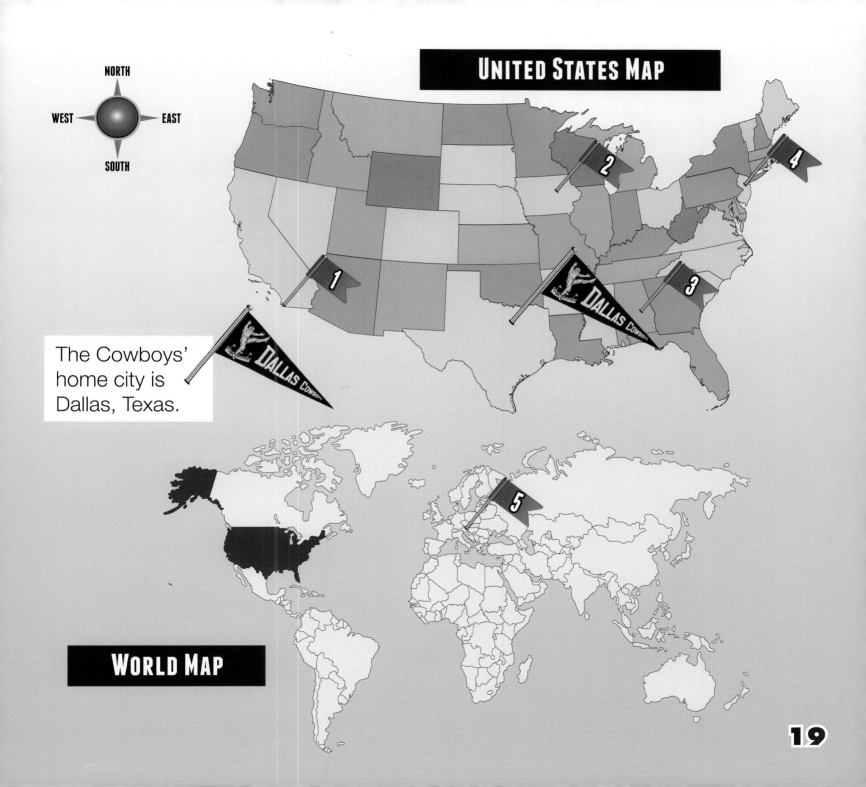

NORTH

WEST ● EAST

SOUTH

The Cowboys' home city is Dallas, Texas.

WORLD MAP

19

HOME AND AWAY

Dez Bryant wears the Cowboys' home uniform.

Football teams wear different uniforms for home and away games. The main colors of the Cowboys are blue, silver, and white. Unlike most NFL teams, Dallas wears white jerseys for home games.

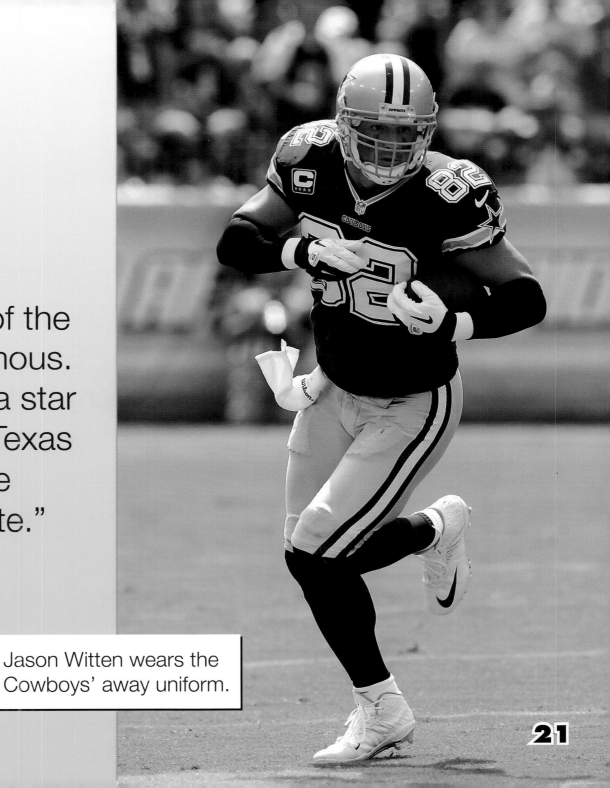

The Cowboys' helmet is one of the NFL's most famous. It is silver with a star on each side. Texas is known as the "Lone Star State."

Jason Witten wears the Cowboys' away uniform.

The Cowboys reached the **playoffs** 18 times from 1966 to 1985. In 1971, **Roger Staubach** led them to their first Super Bowl victory. The Cowboys repeated as champions six years later. They won the Super Bowl three more times in the 1990s.

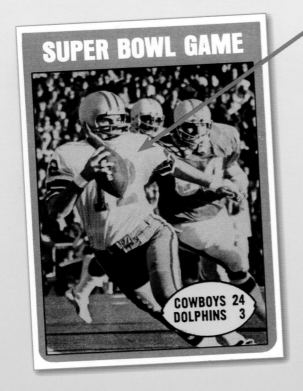

SUPER BOWL GAME

COWBOYS 24
DOLPHINS 3

RECORD BOOK

These Cowboys set team records.

TOUCHDOWN PASSES	RECORD
Season: Tony Romo (2007)	36
Career: Tony Romo	247

TOUCHDOWN CATCHES	RECORD
Season: Dez Bryant (2014)	16
Career: **Bob Hayes**	71

RUSHING YARDS	RECORD
Season: DeMarco Murray (2014)	1,845
Career: Emmitt Smith	17,162

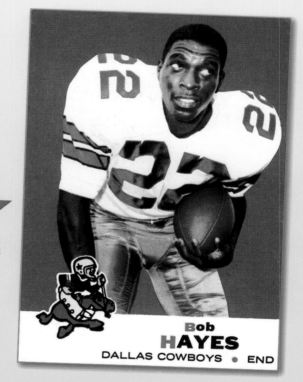

Bob **HAYES**
DALLAS COWBOYS • END

ANSWERS FOR THE BIG PICTURE
The stripe on the pants of the player to the far left changed to gray, #9 changed to #6, and #9's helmet changed to blue.

ANSWER FOR TRUE AND FALSE
#2 is false. Tony's father and grandfather were not real cowboys.

FOOTBALL WORDS

INDEX

All-Pro
An honor given to the best NFL player at each position.

Playoffs
The games played after the regular season that decide which teams will play in the Super Bowl.

Pro Bowl
The NFL's annual all-star game.

Quarterback Sacks
Tackles of the quarterback that lose yardage.

ABOUT THE AUTHOR

Zack Burgess has been writing about sports for more than 20 years. He has lived all over the country and interviewed lots of All-Pro football players, including Brett Favre, Eddie George, Jerome Bettis, Shannon Sharpe, and Rich Gannon. Zack was the first African American beat writer to cover Major League Baseball when he worked for the *Kansas City Star*.

ABOUT THE COWBOYS

Learn more at these websites:
www.dallascowboys.com • www.profootballhof.com
www.teamspiritextras.com/Overtime/html/cowboys.html